CHEROKEE

OCT 4 - 1990

Fire
and Water

Library Edition Published 1990

Published by Marshall Cavendish Corporation
147 West Merrick Road
Freeport, Long Island
N.Y. 11520

Printed in Italy by New Interlitho, Milan

© Marshall Cavendish Limited 1989
© Cherrytree Press Limited 1988

Library Edition produced by DPM Services Limited

Library of Congress Cataloging-in-Publication Data

Kerrod, Robin.
    Fire and water / by Robin Kerrod: illustrated by Mike Atkinson
and Sarah Atkinson.
      p. cm. − (Secrets of science : 2)
    "A Cherrytree book."
    Includes index
    Summary: Projects, activities, and experiments explore different
aspects of fire and water.
    1. Scientific recreations − Juvenile literature. 2. Fire -
Experiment − Juvenile literature. 3. Water − Experiments −
Juvenile
  literature. [1. Scientific recreations. 2. Fire − Experiments.
  3. Water − Experiments. 4. Experiments.]
  I. Atkinson, Mike. [1]. II. Atkinson, Sarah, [1]. III. Title.
  IV. Series: Kerrod, Robin, Secrets of science : 2.
    Q164.K45 1989
    542' − dc19   89-917
                                            CIP
                                            AC

ISBN 1-85435-153-2
ISBN 1-85435-151-6(set)

SECRETS OF SCIENCE
Fire and Water

Robin Kerrod

Illustrated by Mike Atkinson
and Sarah Atkinson

MARSHALL CAVENDISH
NEW YORK · LONDON · TORONTO · SYDNEY

Safety First

☐ Ask an adult for permission before you start any experiment, especially if you are using matches or anything hot, sharp, or poisonous.

☐ Don't wear good clothes. Wear old ones or an apron.

☐ If you work on a table, use an old one and protect it with paper or cardboard.

☐ Do water experiments in the sink, on the draining board, or outdoors.

☐ Strike matches away from your body, and make sure they are out before you throw them away.

☐ Make sure candles are standing securely.

☐ Wear oven gloves when handling anything hot.

☐ Be careful when cutting things. Always cut away from your body.

☐ Don't use tin cans with jagged edges. Use those with lids.

☐ Use only safe children's glue, glue sticks, or paste.

☐ **Never** taste chemicals, unless the book tells you to.

☐ Label all bottles and jars containing chemicals, and store them where young children can't get at them – and never in the family's food cupboard.

☐ Never use or play with electricity. It can KILL. Use a battery to create a current if needed.

☐ When you have finished an experiment, put your things away, clean up, and wash your hands.

Contents

Safety First 4

Useful, but Dangerous 6

Fire! Fire! 8

Snuff It Out 10

Slow Fires 12

Fire and Water Inside 14

Water Power 16

Losing Weight 18

Pumping Water 20

Salty Solutions 22

Crystal Clear 24

Skin Deep 26

Steaming and Freezing 28

Hot & Cold, Heavy & Light 30

Index and Glossary 32

Useful, but Dangerous

Fire and water are useful, but they can be dangerous, so always be careful with them. Ask an adult before you use matches, and never use anything except safety matches. When you want to strike a match, take one from the box, close the box, and strike the match away from you. Don't let it burn down too far. Use it, blow it out quickly, then put it in water. When you use a candle, make sure it is standing firmly on a base. Drip some wax onto the holder first and stick the bottom of the candle into it.

When things burn, they turn to carbon. Light a candle, and look at its flame. You will see two main parts, a darkish area around the wick, and a large yellowish-white part which gives out most of the light. This part of the flame is made up of tiny particles of carbon, which are white-hot.

Push the end of the handle of an old metal spoon into the flame. (Use oven gloves to protect your hands.) When you take the spoon out, the end will be covered with black soot. The soot is carbon, which turns black as it cools.

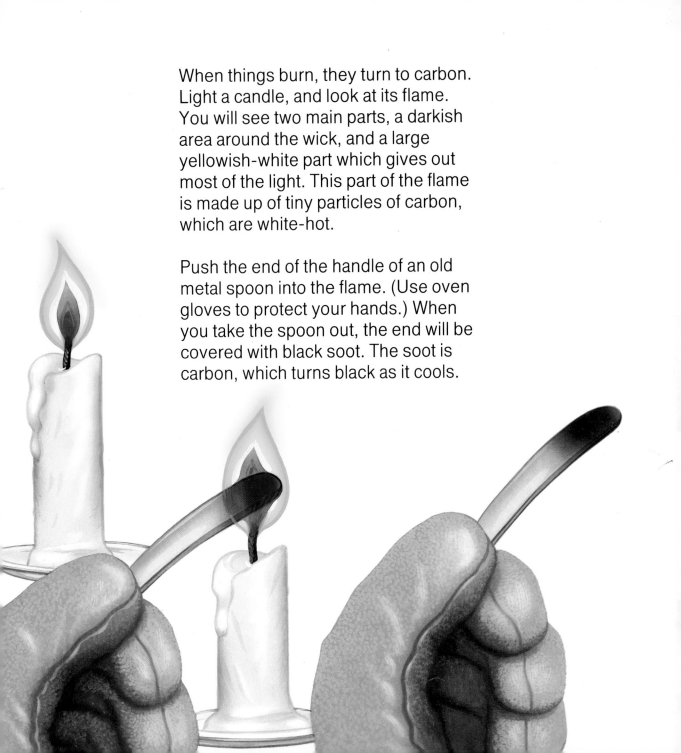

Fire! Fire!

Fire is very much our friend when it is under control. But when it gets out of control, it is a dangerous enemy. Fire needs air to burn. To put out a fire, you must prevent it from getting air. Often, the best way is to throw sand or water on the flames. If an outdoor bonfire gets too fierce, you can smother it with sand or put it out with water from a hose.

Water will not put out all fires. Oil floats on water, so there is no point in using water to try to put out burning oil or grease. The burning oil will simply spatter and float on it.

If a pan of oil or grease catches fire, the best way to put it out is to throw a wet towel over the flames to smother them and stop the air from reaching them. But NEVER set light to oil, even as an experiment. Fire can get out of control in seconds. If that happens, get out of its way as fast as you can, and call for help immediately.

Firemen also use fire extinguishers to put out fires. Many extinguishers produce a gas called carbon dioxide. This gas is heavier than air, and things cannot burn in it. It smothers flames like an invisible blanket.

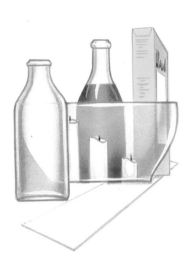

Snuff It Out!

Many home fire extinguishers work by producing carbon dioxide. You can make your own carbon dioxide extinguisher in this experiment.

Making Carbon Dioxide

1 You need a large bowl, three candles of different lengths, stiff paper, glue or tape, a bottle, some baking soda, and some vinegar.

2 Make a paper tube, with an angle in it, which will reach from the bottle to the bowl. The tube should fit the neck of the bottle exactly. (Seal any gaps with modeling clay.)

3 Fix the candles firmly in the bowl and light them.

4 Add a tablespoonful of baking soda to some vinegar in a bottle. Watch how it fizzes and produces gas.

5 Capture the gas in the tube and let it run down the tube into the bowl. See how each candle goes out in turn, as the heavy gas fills the bowl.

When things burn, they use the oxygen in the air. They cannot burn without it. Try this experiment.

Using Oxygen

1 You need a dish of water, a jar, and a candle.

2 Stand the candle firmly in the dish, and pour a little water around it.

3 Light the candle, and put the bottle over it.

4 When it has used up all the oxygen in the air in the bottle, the candle will go out.

5 Observe what has happened to the water. It has risen to take the place of the oxygen.

Slow Fires

You have proved that a candle needs oxygen to burn. As it burns, it combines (joins up) with the oxygen. This process is called **oxidation.**

When fires burn, oxidation takes place quickly, and heat and light are given off. But oxidation can also take place slowly. The rusting of iron is an example of slow oxidation. Iron combines with oxygen in the air to form the orange-brown substance we call rust. Rusting only happens in moist air. Things do not rust if they are kept dry.

If you leave shiny new steel nails outside, they will soon become covered with a thin film of rust. If the nails stay outside for months, they will

become rough. Over a long period of time, they would be completely eaten away by rust.

You can see how rusting uses oxygen in this experiment.

Eating Steel

1 You need some steel wool (a soap-free scouring pad will do), a jar, and a bowl of water.

2 Put some moistened steel wool in the jar.

3 Turn the jar upside down in the bowl of water so that the air is trapped inside.

4 Watch it daily, and observe how the steel wool rusts and turns brown.

5 Watch the water level in the jar. Why does it go up?

before   **after**

Fire and Water Inside

Oxidation also takes place inside our bodies. We eat food to give us energy, and we breathe in oxygen. The food is then "burned" in the oxygen. The slow burning, or oxidation, gives out energy.

Our bodies also contain water. Guess how much? Nearly three-fourths of our weight is water. Without water, we could live for only a few days. In fact, the whole world is very watery. The oceans take up nearly three-fourths of the world's surface.

Have you noticed that the surface of water is always level (except when there are waves)? Water always finds its own level. See for yourself with a length of plastic tube.

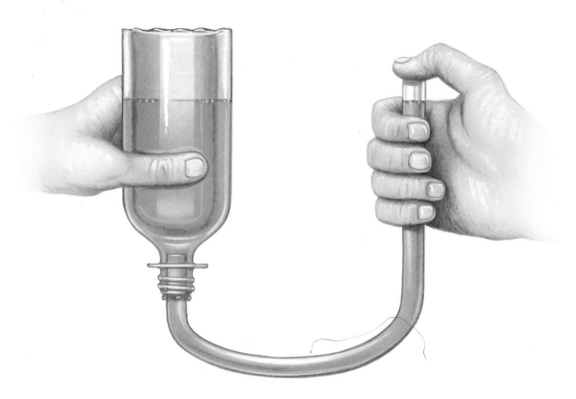

Bottled Up

1 You need a piece of plastic tube, a large plastic soft drink bottle cut in half, and some modeling clay.

2 First, fill the tube half full of water, and place your thumb over one end.

3 Move and coil the tube in different ways. Make sure that the ends of the tube are more or less level and pointing upward. Take your thumb away, and watch what happens to the water levels in the two ends.

4 Now, empty the tube and attach it firmly in the neck of the bottle. Seal it with modeling clay.

5 Fill the bottle and tube with water, keeping your thumb over the end of the tube.

6 Hold the end of the tube above the level of the bottle and take your thumb away. Does the weight of the water in the bottle force the water out of the tube?

Water Power

In the sink, fill up a large plastic soft drink bottle with tap water. Leave the bottle in the sink. Make a hole in the side of the bottle about halfway down with a nail. Stand back as the water spurts out.

Keep the faucet running so that the bottle remains full. Then punch holes above and below the first one. What do you notice about the water spurting out? The water spurts farthest from the bottom hole. This is because the pressure of water becomes greater as you go deeper. That is why dams have to be very thick at the bottom.

Dams are built to store water. Sometimes, the water pressure at the bottom of the dam is used to turn water turbines. The turbines then power generators to make electricity. This is called hydroelectricity. "Hydro" is another word for water.

You can make a water turbine.

Spin It

1 You need a cork with a hole bored in it, a long nail or knitting needle, scissors, and a yogurt pot.

2 Carefully cut six narrow slots at regular intervals in the side of the cork.

3 Push the nail through the hole in the cork.

4 Cut strips from the yogurt pot and wedge them into the slots in the cork.

5 Hold your turbine under the faucet. The running water hits the blades and makes the whole turbine spin.

Losing Weight

Do you know the best way to lose weight? Jump into the water. See how it holds you up. An ancient Greek scientist named Archimedes discovered this while he was having a bath. He jumped out and ran into the street, shouting "Eureka! Eureka! (I've got it! I've got it!)"

Instead of jumping into your bathtub, try "bathing" a brick and a piece of wood. Tie a heavy stone or brick on a piece of string

and lower it into a bucket of water. What do you notice as the brick goes in? Suddenly, it feels lighter. This is because the water is pushing upwards on it.

Now, try the same thing with a piece of wood and see what happens. The wood loses all its weight and floats. The upward force (push) of the water is greater than the downward force (weight) of the wood. You can feel the upward force if you push the wood deeper into the water with your hand.

If you throw a ball of clay into the water, it will sink. It is denser (heavier) than the water. But, if you mold it into a boat shape, it will float. Now, the clay is lighter (less dense) than the same volume of water.

Pumping Water

When you pump up the tires on a bike, you squeeze more and more air into them. You compress the air. But you cannot compress water or other liquids. You can prove this with a bicycle pump.

Put the bottom of the pump in a bowl of water and slowly pull back the handle. The water is drawn into the pump. Now, press a finger over the hole in the bottom, and push down on

the handle. You cannot move it, can you? When you take your finger away, the water will spurt out in a powerful jet.

You can use the fact that air can be compressed and water cannot to make a little diver.

Make a Deep-jar Diver

1 You need a tall jar, a miniature bottle, an old balloon, and some string.

2 Fill the jar with water right up to the brim.

3 Fill the miniature bottle half full of water, and put it upside down in the big jar so that it does not quite sink.

4 Stretch a thin piece of rubber from the balloon over the neck of the jar and tie it in place.

5 Press down on the rubber, and the little bottle will dive. Take your hand away, and the bottle will rise again. Can you see how it works?

Salty Solutions

If you stir a teaspoonful of salt into a glass of water, the salt disappears. You cannot see it, but you can taste it. The salt dissolves in the water to make a solution. See how much you can add to the water before no more will dissolve. Repeat the experiment with hot water. Can you add more or less salt than before?

Water dissolves lots of household things. Try making solutions with sugar, washing powder, and baking soda, – but not all together!

If you had a glass of water and a glass of salty water, could you tell the difference without tasting? You could if you had a hydrometer. A hydrometer measures the density of liquids. It tells how heavy they are. A solution is always more dense than plain water.

Make a Hydrometer

1 You need a straw, some clay, a full glass of water, and other identical glasses full of solutions to test.

2 Stick a little piece of clay on the end of the straw so that it floats in the glass of water.

3 Mark on the straw to show where the water level is.

4 Your hydrometer is now ready. If you place it in a salt solution, it will not sink as low as it does in water. Test your other solutions to see how dense they are.

Crystal Clear

You can make salt disappear in water. But how can you make it reappear? Make a strong salt solution, and pour some of it into a saucer. Leave it somewhere warm, and see how it dries up, or evaporates. Eventually, all the water disappears. But notice what is left; dry, white specks of salt.

You can use a similar method to grow crystals. The minerals that make up rocks often form crystals of many different shapes. See if you can find some like the ones below in hollows in rocks and stones.

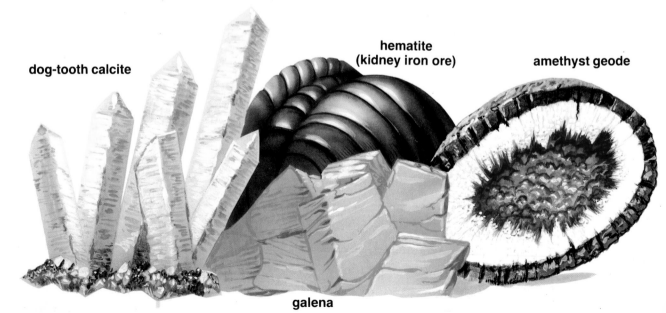

dog-tooth calcite

hematite (kidney iron ore)

amethyst geode

galena

You can grow crystals with salt, sugar, bath salts, and Epsom salts; or you can buy other safe chemicals from the drugstore. Alum is a good one to try.

Growing Crystals

1 You need a jar, hot water, a pitcher, a pencil, some thread, and some alum (or another chemical).

2 In the pitcher, dissolve as much alum as you can in enough hot water to fill the jar half full.

3 Let it cool, and pour the clear liquid into the jar.

4 Tie a piece of thread to a pencil and dangle it down to touch the surface of the solution.

5 Place the jar where it cannot be disturbed, and look at it every day. A small crystal will start to grow on the end of the thread. It will grow bigger and more beautiful each day. Notice how regular its shape is.

Skin Deep

Fill a glass to the brim with water. Then, gently, add more water, a drop at a time. You can add water until the surface is actually above the top of the glass. It seems as if there is a kind of skin on the water. In fact, there is. It is caused by the way water particles pull inward at the surface. We call this pulling force **surface tension.**

Add a drop of liquid detergent to the glass, and watch the skin collapse. The water spills out of the glass. The liquid detergent lowers the surface tension.

Soap also lowers surface tension. Cut a piece of cardboard into a boat shape and try to "sail" it on the water. Wedge a small piece of soap at the back, and watch your boat streak away.

Water also rises in small tubes. Fill a clean ketchup bottle with water and watch the water in the neck curve up at the edges. Then, drop a transparent straw into the neck. You can see the water in the straw rise above the level of the water in the neck. This effect is called **capillarity**. The narrow spaces between the grains in a lump of sugar act like little tubes. So do the tiny holes in a towel. That is why they can soak up liquids – by capillarity.

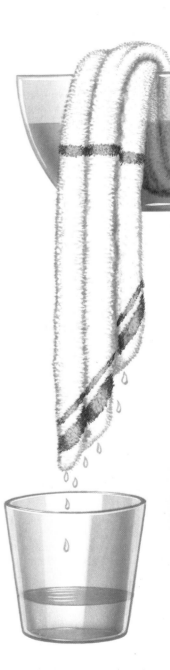

Steaming and Freezing

If you leave water in a saucer for a while, it evaporates. It changes into a **vapor** (gas) and becomes invisible. Water changes into vapor much more quickly when it is boiled. It boils when the temperature reaches 212 degrees F (Fahrenheit). When it boils, you see bubbles of vapor forming and bursting out into the air. You also see steam rising. Steam is a cloud of tiny droplets of water. The droplets form when the hot vapor hits the colder air and changes back into water.

Water vapor in the air also changes back into liquid water when it comes up against a cold surface. The bathroom or

kitchen windows sometimes get steamed up on a cold day and even start trickling water.

On really cold days, you may find solid water on the windows in the form of ice. Water freezes, or turns into ice, when its temperature falls to 32 degrees F. When water freezes, it expands or gets bigger. See this for yourself.

Smashing Ice

1 You need an unwanted test tube with a cork, a strong plastic bag, some water, and a refrigerator or freezer.

2 Fill the test tube with water and cork it.

3 Seal it inside the plastic bag and leave it overnight in the freezer.

4 In the morning, remove the bag carefully, and see what has happened! Be very careful with the broken glass.

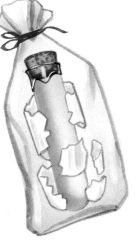

Hot & Cold, Heavy & Light

Do you know what happens to water when you heat it? Fill a bottle to the brim with cold water, and then pour the water into a saucepan. Heat it up, but do not boil it. Now, pour it all back into the bottle. You can't, can you? There is some hot water left over. This is because the water has expanded. It has become lighter, or less dense.

Here are two clever tricks to end with!

Jumping Water

1 You need two jars with mouths the same size, a piece of cardboard, and some colored ink.

2 Fill one jar with hot tap water, and add ink to it until it is quite a dark color.

3 Fill the other jar to the brim with cold water and place the cardboard over it.

4 Now carefully turn the cold jar upside down, and place it exactly over the mouth of the hot jar.

5 Carefully slide the cardboard out from between the jars, and watch what happens to the hot inky water.

Dancing Mothballs

1 You need a large jar, vinegar, baking soda, and a few mothballs.

2 Fill your jar with water, and drop the mothballs into the water. They are denser (heavier) than water, so they sink.

3 Take the mothballs out and slowly stir in a few tablespoonfuls of vinegar and baking soda.

4 Now, drop the mothballs in again, and watch them dance up to the surface and down again.

5 Can you think why the mothballs are now dancing? The baking soda and vinegar give off carbon dioxide gas. Bubbles of the gas cling to the balls and make them light enough to float. When they reach the surface, the bubbles burst, and the balls become heavy enough to sink again.

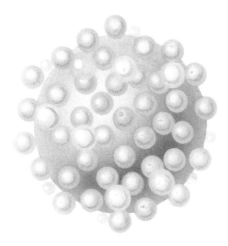

Index and Glossary

alum 25
  a salt that forms beautiful crystals
amethyst 24
  a kind of quartz (mineral)
Archimedes 18

bicycle pump 20
boiling water 28
bonfire 8
burning 8, 12, 13

calcite 24
  a crystal form of chalk (mineral)
candles 6, 7
capillarity 27
carbon 7
carbon dioxide 9-11, 31
  a heavy gas often used in fire extinguishers to put out fires
Cartesian diver, see diver
compressing air 20, 21
crystals 24, 25
  the geometric shapes minerals and salts often form

dams 16, 17
  structures built to hold back water
dancing mothballs 31
density 23, 24, 30

the weight of something compared with the weight of the same volume of water
dissolve 22
  what happens to a substance like salt when it is stirred into water and disappears
diver 21

fire 8, 9
fire extinguisher 9, 10
flame 7
  the light given out when something burns
floating 19
freezing water 29

galena 24
  a lead mineral
growing crystals 25

hot and cold 28-31
hydroelectricity 17
  electricity produced by harnessing the energy of flowing water
hydrometer 23
  an instrument that measures the density of a liquid

ice 29

jumping water 30

kidney iron ore 24
  an iron oxide mineral

matches 6
minerals 24
  the chemical substances that make up rocks

oil fire 8, 9
oxidation 12, 14
  the chemical reaction that takes place when substances combine with the oxygen in the air
oxygen 11-14

pump 20

rusting 12, 13
  what happens when iron is left out in damp air. It combines with the oxygen in the air to form a powder.

safety matches 6
  matches that can be struck only on a special surface
salt 22, 24
salts 25
sinking 19, 31

slow fire 12
soap and surface tension 26, 27
solution 22, 24, 25
  water that contains something dissolved in it
soot 7
steam 28
  a cloud made up of little droplets of water, formed when hot water vapor cools in the air
surface tension 26, 27
  a force on the surface of a liquid that gives it a kind of skin

water and fire 8
water in the body 14
water in the earth 14
water levels 14, 15
water pressure 16, 17
  the force water exerts on each square inch of something placed in it. It increases with depth.
water turbine 17
  a machine spun by flowing water
water vapor 28
  water in the form of a gas
weight in water 18, 19